BE YOUR BEST

GRATITUDE

Shannon Welbourn

www.av2books.com

Step 1
Go to www.av2books.com

Step 2
Enter this unique code

DLCMQVCMD

Step 3
Explore your interactive eBook!

AV2 is optimized for use on any device

Your interactive eBook comes with...

Contents
Browse a live contents page to easily navigate through resources

Audio
Listen to sections of the book read aloud

Videos
Watch informative video clips

Weblinks
Gain additional information for research

Try This!
Complete activities and hands-on experiments

Key Words
Study vocabulary, and complete a matching word activity

Quizzes
Test your knowledge

Slideshows
View images and captions

... and much, much more!

View new titles and product videos at www.av2books.com

BE YOUR BEST

GRATITUDE

Contents

4	What Is Gratitude?
6	Why Is Gratitude Important?
8	Biography: Taylor Swift
10	Gratitude at Home
12	Gratitude at School
14	Gratitude in Your Community
16	Case Study: Pay It Forward Day
18	Overcoming Challenges
20	Encouraging Gratitude in Others
22	Grow Your Gratitude
23	Key Words/Index

What Is Gratitude?

Do you know which two words are so powerful they can make you feel happier just by saying them? These two words are thank you!

We say thank you when someone does something kind or helpful. Saying thank you is one way to show gratitude. Gratitude is being aware of and thankful for the people, experiences, and things in our lives. These words show that we feel **grateful** for what they have done. Feeling grateful is also feeling happy about something good that has happened.

Gratitude is an attitude, or way of thinking, that everyone can learn. Like learning anything new, it takes time and practice. Gratitude changes the way you see the world. It can help you at home, in school, and other areas of your life.

We can show gratitude by saying thank you or by doing something nice for someone.

People who show gratitude are thankful for the everyday things and experiences in their lives.

Why Is Gratitude Important?

Gratitude makes people feel happy because they are aware of and appreciate the people and things around them.

You can build gratitude by learning to be **mindful**. Being mindful means paying close attention to what is happening right now. Often, people think about things that happened in the past, or things that will happen in the future. Being mindful helps you discover wonderful new things to be grateful for in the present moment. When you are with friends, try paying close attention to the funny stories they tell and how much they make you laugh. You will feel even more grateful that you are friends!

Being mindful helps your gratitude grow!

Be Your Best

Gratitude helps us appreciate the good things in our lives. It encourages us to give back to others.

Think of a time that someone showed you gratitude. How did it make you feel? Gratitude helps us feel closer and more connected to our families and friends. Being mindful and appreciating the things around you also helps connect you to your **community** and the people in it.

BIOGRAPHY

Taylor Swift

Showing gratitude is important for everyone, even people who seem to have all that they could ever want!

Taylor Swift is a famous musician. She is very talented, but her success also comes from how well she treats her millions of fans around the world. Taylor's fans support her by listening to her music, buying tickets to her concerts, and following her on **social media**. Taylor feels grateful to her fans because they made her success possible.

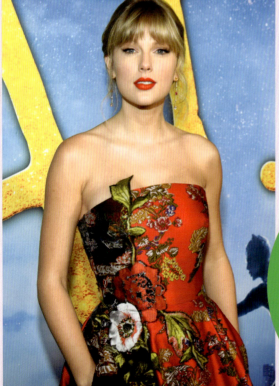

NAME: **Taylor Swift**
FROM: **Wyomissing, Pennsylvania**
ACCOMPLISHMENT: **Shows her gratitude to her fans every day**

Taylor Swift was only **16** years old when her first album came out.

Taylor has more than 290 million followers on social media. She follows many of them back and often gives them words of encouragement!

The Taylor Swift Education Center opened in **2013** in Nashville, Tennessee, to teach people about **music**.

She shows her gratitude in many different ways, including mailing letters and gifts to fans, and showing up at their birthday parties and events. She makes time to meet her fans to take pictures and chat with them.

In 2020, Taylor helped a fan who lost her job by sending her **$3,000**.

Gratitude

Gratitude at Home

What are you grateful to have in your home life?

Parents or other adults that care for us work hard to provide food, shelter, and other **basic needs**. We might not think about these things as often as we should. Saying thank you will make the people who work hard to care for you feel that you appreciate all that they do. When we thank someone, it is not enough to just say those two words. It is important to tell them what we are grateful for, such as telling your sister you are grateful that she helps you with your homework. Try practicing gratitude with your family by sitting together and telling each other reasons you are thankful.

Go around the table and say one thing you are grateful for that happened during the day, and then one reason you are grateful for a family member. This can help you and your family to be mindful of all the reasons you have to be grateful at home.

Learn to Make Decisions

Think of a reason you are grateful for each member of your family. Share your gratitude with them!

Gratitude 11

Gratitude at School

There are many reasons to show gratitude at school. Being able to go to school is something to be grateful for.

Some children around the world cannot go to school because they have to work to help support their families. Other children may have to travel far from their home to attend school.

These students in Somalia do not always have enough **resources**, such as books and computers, to use at school—but they are grateful to go to school.

Think about all of the resources you use at school. You write with pens and pencils, study from books, and work on computers. You have a desk and a classroom to learn in. These are all things to be grateful for.

Maybe you are grateful for a teacher you really like, or a favorite subject to study. Does a bus driver get you safely to and from school? Does a school nurse help you feel better when you are sick? Making the decision to be thankful for the things you have at school helps you build gratitude.

Gratitude in Your Community

A community is a group of people who live, work, and play in a place. Your home, school, and neighborhood are part of your community.

It is important to show gratitude for the experiences you have in your community, such as playing sports. You should be mindful of the people who make your community a good place to live, such as doctors who care for you and postal service workers who deliver your mail.

Maybe you take lessons to learn something new. You can be grateful for the opportunity to try new things or learn more about something you already enjoy.

You can also show gratitude for the places in your community. Be mindful of the natural world around you, such as plants and animals that live in your community. You can show your gratitude for your community by **respecting** the natural world. You can also develop gratitude by visiting quiet places in your community to **reflect** on things you are thankful for. A calm, quiet space such as a park can be the perfect place to develop mindfulness and realize your appreciation for the places in your community.

> Show your gratitude for your community by respecting the places, people, and other living things within it.

CASE STUDY

Pay It Forward Day

Often, people who are grateful for the good in their lives also do things to help others. They do not expect anything in return. They are inspired to help, and it makes them feel good to help others.

Pay It Forward Day gives everyone a chance to show their gratitude by helping others. Anyone can take part. All you need is an attitude for gratitude! On Pay It Forward Day, people show their gratitude by doing a good deed for someone and expecting nothing in return. The person who was helped by the good deed is encouraged to "pay it forward" through another good deed. This spreads gratitude far and wide!

NAME: Pay It Forward Day
FROM: Began in Australia, spread worldwide
ACCOMPLISHMENT: Encourages millions of people to show gratitude

Be Your Best

The good deeds can be big or small. To show your gratitude, you can choose any good deed to do for any person you wish. Every helpful act counts! You do not need to wait for the next Pay it Forward Day. Here are some good deeds you might try.

- Help your brother with his paper route.
- Bring your friends study notes when they are sick and miss class.
- Water the garden for your grandpa.
- Prepare lunch for your teacher or parent.

Pay It Forward Day was created in 2007.

Pay It Forward Day is celebrated every year on **April 28th.** APRIL 28

More than **85** countries around the world celebrate Pay It Forward Day.

Overcoming Challenges

When we face problems or challenges, it can be difficult to remember to show gratitude for the things we have.

Being grateful can be challenging when we feel discouraged, angry, or worried. For example, if you are arguing with your brother or sister about what to watch on television, it can be easy to forget how grateful you felt when he or she helped you clean your room earlier in the day. Remembering reasons why you are grateful for people can help you overcome arguments.

Gratitude encourages forgiveness! Next time you have an argument, think of a reason why you are grateful for that person.

When we experience challenges, we sometimes feel discouraged. Maybe your piano teacher was disappointed with you when you forgot to practice a new song for your lesson. The lesson was more difficult because you were not prepared. Sometimes, we may not feel grateful for an experience at the time it happens, but we can look back later and see how it has helped us. That difficult piano lesson may have made you realize how helpful it is to be prepared. Now, you always make sure to take time to practice.

Learn to Make Decisions

Think back to a challenge you faced. Think of a reason you can be grateful for it.

Gratitude 19

Encouraging Gratitude in Others

Being aware of your own gratitude helps you be happier. You can be a reason why someone else feels grateful, too!

Think of a way that you have thanked someone. When you show your gratitude to others, you encourage them to also **express** when they are thankful. Help others think of reasons why they are grateful for the people, experiences, and things in their lives. Encourage them to be mindful and appreciate everything they already have. Explain the reasons why you are grateful for others. Tell them how they make you feel. Then, "pay it forward" by doing something nice for them, and be a reason why they are grateful!

Learn to Make Decisions

Together with friends, come up with a list of reasons why you are thankful for each other.

Grow Your Gratitude

One way to grow your gratitude is to show your gratitude!

It is important to take the time to show your gratitude to the people who deserve it. You may think that people already know how much you appreciate them. What if they do not? By taking the time to show your gratitude, you can be sure people know how you feel.

NAME THE PERSON
Think of all the people who care about you and help you reach your goals. These people may include family members, teachers, friends, tutors, and coaches.

YOU CHOOSE
You can show your gratitude in different ways. For example, you can tell the person, write a letter, make a card, sing a song, or write a poem. The choice is yours!

BE SPECIFIC
No matter how you choose to show your gratitude, you must be specific. Saying thank you is a good start, but it is important to describe the reasons why you are grateful. Think about:
- What did the person do?
- How did they help you or make a difference?

Key Words

appreciate: to feel or show thanks
basic needs: the things, such as food, shelter, and water, that a person needs to survive, or stay alive
community: a group of people who live, work, and play in a place
express: to state something aloud, in words
grateful: thankful or appreciative
mindful: describing someone who is attentive, aware, or careful of what is going on around them

reflect: to think back on something
resources: supplies or support needed to do something
respecting: giving something or someone the attention it deserves
social media: websites or applications where people share information and communicate with each other

Index

basic needs 10

community 7, 9, 14, 15

home 4, 10, 11, 12, 14

mindful 6, 7, 11, 14, 15, 20

Pay It Forward Day 16, 17

reflect 15

school 4, 12, 13, 14
Swift, Taylor 8, 9

Get the best of both worlds.
AV2 bridges the gap between print and digital.

The expandable resources toolbar enables quick access to content including **videos**, **audio**, **activities**, **weblinks**, **slideshows**, **quizzes**, and **key words**.

Animated videos make static images come alive.

Resource icons on each page help readers to further **explore key concepts**.

Published by AV2
350 5th Avenue, 59th Floor
New York, NY 10118
Website: www.av2books.com

Copyright ©2021 AV2
All rights reserved. No part of this publication may be reproduced, stored in a retrieval system, or transmitted in any form or by any means, electronic, mechanical, photocopying, recording, or otherwise, without the prior written permission of the publisher.

Library of Congress Control Number: 2020937051

ISBN 978-1-7911-3154-8 (Hardcover)
ISBN 978-1-7911-3155-5 (Softcover)
ISBN 978-1-7911-3156-2 (Multi-user eBook)
ISBN 978-1-7911-3157-9 (Single-user eBook)

Printed in Guangzhou, China
1 2 3 4 5 6 7 8 9 0   24 23 22 21 20

042020
101119

Project Coordinator: Sara Cucini   Designer: Jean Faye Marie Rodriguez

Every reasonable effort has been made to trace ownership and to obtain permission to reprint copyright material. The publishers would be pleased to have any errors or omissions brought to their attention so that they may be corrected in subsequent printings.

Weigl acknowledges iStock, Getty Images, and Shutterstock as its primary image suppliers for this title.

First published by Crabtree Publishing Company in 2017.

View new titles and product videos at www.av2books.com